Beautiful Reminders

Anew

Banafsheh Akhlaghi

Published by
Hasmark Publishing
1-888-402-0027 ext 101

Disclaimer
The author has done her best to present accurate and up-to-date information in this book, but cannot guarantee that the information is correct or will suit your particular situation. Further, the publisher has used its best efforts in preparing this book, and the information provided herein is provided "as is."

Cover design by NZ Graphics
www.nzgraphics.com

Book layout by DocUmeant Designs
www.documeantdesigns.com

First Edition, 2015

ISBN: 978-0-9920116-0-4
ISBN: 0992011604

Dedication

This book is dedicated to our collective humanity as we continue our journey on the path of evolving our consciousness.

Blessed be you and yours, dear ones.

Contents

Introduction

This book is meant for reading out loud. It is in the hearing of your voice reciting the words that you will connect to the vibration behind each intention.

Reading *Beautiful Reminders* to a loved one, such as yourself, will grant you the ability to hear each message. This process will provide you with the allowance to invite the sentiment into your being, into your heart.

I send to you my gratitude for your willingness to embark upon this journey, leading you back to your highest and greatest Self.

Enjoy dear ones.

Beautiful Reminders

Our life flows similar to moving water.

We glide around obstructions,
dance with neighboring elements
to a harmonious rhythm
and reflect our true essence
through the glistening
of the rays that feed us.

We are clear and free.

It's our journey to wash over,
our path to direct.

Flow with ease.

*Embrace the movement and
surrender into it, dear ones.*

Iao Valley State Park
Wailuku, Hawaii

The glisten of life is before us
in each moment.

Capture it.

The rapture of nature's grandeur
is within us.

Celebrate it.

The manifestation of our happiness
is ours.

Create it.

It's your day to capture,
create and celebrate.

Blessings to you, dear ones.

Anahola Beach Park
Kapaa, Hawaii

Piazza San Marco
Venice, Italy

The arc of life.

We may not know where
our individual pinnacle point lies
on the lifeline of our path.

It may be behind us, waiting for us,
or right here and now.

Go on, go on, and turn the corner.

It's nothing to fear.

It's the wisdom of the ages that
is waiting for you, dear.
The tenderness of ancestors.

Go on; go on walk towards it
with your arms wide open and
your heart ready for its embrace.

It's the path designated to you,
your ultimate grace.

Looking for a love affair?

Be the one you are looking to love
and
watch the magic unveil around you.

Have a love bound day, dear ones.

A new day is before you.

New thoughts emerging into
new words,
flowing and yielding new actions.

Allow the new day to embrace you.

Allow the new breath to guide you.

Allow the glowing magnificence of
your spirit to shine through you.

Blessings dear ones.

Hanalei Bay
Kauai, Hawaii

Trust that where you are,
at this moment,
this very one, is perfect.

Resisting the moment
has us resisting the perfection
of our life.

It's in the stillness,
ease from judging and comparing,
where our next steps reveal themselves.

It's in the dance with life that
the next harmonious sway
will take us to the next and next,
gracefully.

And through the process
please remember,
your life is sheer perfection
because *You* are.

Blessings dear ones.

Kauai's Hindu Monastery
Kapaa, Hawaii

Full circle.

With patience and grace,
a sobering reality welcomes us.

A reality where love and beauty
are the main ingredients
of a fulfilling life.

Where happiness and joyful ease are
the cornerstones and
the foundation.

Not much more complex than that...
not more differing than that.

*May you be blissed out and peacefully
in the state of love, dear ones.*

Puu Poa Beach
Princeville, Hawaii

And so it is when the arc of life bends
and carries us into *another direction*...

Sometimes we go willingly,
as to be carried...

Sometimes we go in reluctance,
as to create struggle.

Nonetheless, we go.

Blessings dear ones.

Santa Fe Train Depot
San Diego, California

Ke'e Beach
Kauai, Hawaii

There is that precious moment in life
when it all makes sense.
And then it's gone again.

Only to know that it will return and
vanish once more.

Yes, it is the ebb and flow of life.

The relinquishing of control.

That is The Precious Moment.

*Blessings on the creation of
your precious moment, dear ones.*

Florence, Italy

Treasured is the infinite beauty
surrounding us each day.

It's my gift to see, feel, and allow it
to wash over me
while in the foreground
I witness the shadow aspects
of our humanity.

The Yang to the Yin.

Balance.

Perspective.

It's all part of the whole.
Focusing on the light first,
and knowing
the shadow comes along side,
everything.

Sending you abundant love dear ones.

It's one of those days
when it all makes sense.

The family and the beloved,
the friends and the career,
the health and finances,
the contribution and spirituality.

One of those rare days
when all aspects of life
have that particular quality
of restfulness.

The quality that
life is going as it should be
and there is order and calm.

Not every day,
or every moment within a day,
is present with this gift, this knowing,
exuding within me.

Stinson Beach, California

But on this day, I celebrate
the peacefullness of my life.

*My loving blessings to each of you
dear ones, on this peaceful path
called your life.*

Here we go, dear ones,
the day is upon us.

Here's to a playfully intoxicating,
peacefully productive,
tantalizingly memorable time before us.

Let's play it all out.

You know all those items we say
we'll get to, someday, maybe,
but not right now?

Those ones... yes those.

Whether it's spending time with your
loved ones, going to that special place
in nature, or checking off another item
on your bucket list...
let's have a splendidly spectacular time
being in our lives.

It's all ours after all.

Blessings and love to each of you.

Japanese Garden, The Butchart Gardens
Brentwood Bay, British Columbia, Canada

Victoria Inner Harbor
Vancouver Island, British Columbia, Canada

A moment of stillness.

A whisper of softness.

A lifetime of access to the inner voice.

Blessings dear ones.

As the river bends,
so does our life's path.

Not knowing exactly what
is around the corner.

Always trusting in the process
and knowing we are taken care of.

*Blessings on your day with every twist
and turn ahead, dear ones.*

Arno River
Florence, Italy

It's simple...

We all know failure is part of life.

We all know
if we haven't failed
we aren't playing
a big enough game in life.

One worthy of who we are meant to be
in this lifetime.

We all know that failures are not
forever, and merely a transition
—a temporary condition—
for that moment in time,
and then a new moment arises
giving rise for success.

But we tend to forget....

Here's to our reminder; failures are a
human condition, welcomed,
and the prelude to your
next successful moment.

Blessings dear ones.

Turtle Bay Beach
Kahuku, Hawaii

Liberate yourself
through freeing up your hearts
from past chains, and while there,
release the thoughts
that accompany those feelings.

Make it a soaring, freeing kind of day,
dear ones.

Love wins.

It does every time.

Sunken Garden, Butchart Gardens
Brentwood Bay, British Columbia, Canada

Interdependence / interconnectedness,
the glue is always ... Love.

One voice. One breath.
It is the truth that unites us all.

The challenge is remembering this
when one is harsh and war creating
towards one's self and others.

It's in those moments,
with those individuals,
that the opportunity is presented
to see
where I am harsh and
where I am war creating with another.

We are One.

Love and compassion are the very
essence of me, the very essence of you,
the very essence of what we call
the other.

It's the path, dear ones.

Ripples of our lives
reach far, and yet near.

Our love's force
is ours to share,
only for the love
to be replenished
from the action of giving,
witnessing the receiving,
and always knowing
it is vast and abundant
in form and nature.

Ours is to love.

Ours is to produce love.

Ours is to inhale the love
surrounding us.

*Wish you a day filled
with being in love,
dear ones.*

Anahola Beach Park
Kapaa, Hawaii

May we surrender to tenderness,
compassion and love.

May we provide allowance
for friendship,
authentic communication,
and contribution for ourselves,
and for others.

May we live fully today and everyday.

Have a blessedly sweet day, dear ones.

May we be blessed this day
with the sight to see
the moment beyond this one
while being present
to this moment.

May we be blessed with the courage
to hear the gifts spoken from
the universe contributing to us,
while playfully laughing
each day.

With my love to each of you,
dear ones.

Butchart Gardens
Brentwood Bay, British Columbia, Canada

Hanalei Pier
Hanalei, Hawaii

Awaken from the slumber.

Bewitched by the rise.

Dance to the melody of life.

Move,

Flow,

Breath

as if it were your time.

Your time
and yours alone
to shine.

Shine bright dear ones.

Choose to dance barefoot,
skip and glide freely.

May your moments be filled with
a sense of curiosity and play,
regardless of your age.

Blessings of joy to you dear ones.

Hanalei Bay Beach
Hanalei, Hawaii

Remember that dream that light's up your heart, keep moving toward it.

One day you will look around to see you are swimming within it, fully manifested.

Blessings dear ones.

La Sagrada Família Church
Barcelona, Spain

Lean back...

    far back...

        into your Self.

Allow rest and solace
to be your companions.

Hush the world outside of you
for even a moment,
to catch your breath,
and you soul's desire.

Breathe in your magnificence.

Go on.

Breathe in
Your
purity and strength.

Emboldened,
walk into your day.

Blessings dear ones.

Villa & Jardins Ephrussi de Rothchild
St. Jean-Cap-Ferrat, France

Hanalei Bay Resort
Princeville, Hawaii

Here is to a new day, dear ones.

A day waiting to be discovered.

A day not like any other before it.

A day we get to create
our conclusion to,
write the ending of,
bask in the contentment for
who we were
through the events before us.

Here is to your new day.

With love and blessings, dear ones.

Today
and
every day,
find a way
for the
Truth of Yourself
to express
Itself.

Your stage of life awaits
your best performance yet.

You have written the script,
you have cast all the actors,
and you know how it ends.

There is only one aspect
left to remember,
have fun
and
enjoy the process.

Blessings dear ones!

Spreckels Temple of Music, Golden Gate Park
San Francisco, California

The light of *lights* is yours.

Shine your soul's light
to the world surrounding you.

Shine your light
toward the darkness
and watch the power
of your inner light
cast truth,
warmth,
and love
to those areas that are
dormant,
stagnate, or hopeless.

Anahola Beach Park
Kapaa, Hawaii

Shine your heart's desires
towards life's wonder
and dreams of the impossible.

Shine, dear ones, shine.

Rose Garden, Butchart Gardens
Brentwood Bay, British Columbia, Canada

My mouth is the paintbrush,
and my words are the paint.

The power of the spoken word.

If we only *really* got,
how powerful our words are
in creating our world around us,
we would be more accountable
with the words we choose.

The words we select to use,
shape everything in our reality.

Be mindful with your word
about yourself, others, and the world.

Then step back and witness
how your words start
to produce outcomes
you are intending.

Blessings dear ones.

Italian Garden, Butchart Gardens
Brentwood Bay, British Columbia, Canada

There hasn't been a mistake made.

There isn't another life waiting
for you around the corner.

This is it.

The one you are waiting for.

The one you've been granted.

Live it fully expressed.

Live it out loud.

Live it with peaceful embrace.

Live it my dear ones, live it now.

Discovery in life!

Fall into what awaits.

Allow it to carry you
into a new experience,
with
new *thoughts,*
new *words,*
new *actions,*
to produce
New Results.

*Blessings on a joyfilled day,
dear ones.*

Lake Tahoe, California

The day breaks
with a bit of dew in the air.

The breeze welcomes a new day
to each living being.

We are here, ready, and passionate.

We are present, capable, and embraced.

We are life.

Here is to life, with peacefulness.

Blessings dear ones.

The Grand Canal
Venice, Italy

So here it is:

If you feel at times
you are living a scene
out of the movie
Groundhog Day,
it's time to put
the past into the past.

Nothing new
is going to come
from the past...
really,
it's how it works.

Yosemite National Park
Yosemite Village, California

Our reflection,
our footprint,
our impact
is grand.

Our awareness on
how we leave others,
the planet,
and ourselves
after each encounter
brings to light a query.

"What am I committed to creating
with my *thoughts,*
my *words,*
my *deeds?"*

*May your light shine through you
and beyond you, loved ones.
Wishing you a reflective day.*

It's but
ONE
moment
and then
another arises.

It always does.

The sun is shining.

The brightness of life is lit.

Come on, come out
from around the shield.

Nothing here to protect from.

Nothing here to fear.

There is a treasured moment,
a gift, which awaits.

Come on, come out
from around the doubt and worry.

Allow the rays of the sun,
the light breeze upon your skin,
and the sound of the dancing leaves
presence the life ahead.

Come on, come out dear ones.

St. Regis Hotel, Hanalei Bay
Princeville, Hawaii

Truly a gift
to graciously provide a *listening*
—really hearing—
another as grand,
magnificent,
and a highly capable
Being.

To be heard in this way,
while the other clearly knows of the
weaknesses of being human,
provides the space to know oneself
with all that we are
and all that we are not.

A generous treasure to be heard
by another
free from judgment and
filled with liberation.

May each of you bestow this gift
upon another and may you be
the receiver of the same.

Blessed be your day, dear ones.

St. Regis Hotel Lanai
Princeville, Hawaii

Hiram M. Chittenden Locks
Seattle, Washington

As the water flows without obstruction,
so shall their words and opinions.

If they talk about you,
whether highly or poorly,
it's not of your concern rather theirs.

If they try to undermine or build you up,
it's not of your concern rather theirs.

If they campaign with a sense to diminish or
rave about your work,
your commitment, your contribution,
or your presence,
it's not of your concern rather theirs.

You see my dear,
they communicate from their own
reflections of realities, not the truth.
Your truth is the one deep within you. Quiet
and still within your soul.
That voice matters.
That's where reality meets the truth.

So let them talk, doubt, rave, or engage for
You know You. Let their realities flow and
run down the river of life to meet up
with all of those that went before them.

It's not of your concern rather theirs.

As out-of-reach the dream may feel...

As unattainable others may say
your dreams are...

As foolish as you may feel
to keep believing in those dreams...

As challenged and challenging the road
behind you may be...

Somewhere deep within you,
you know.

You know this dream is
to live outside of you,
because it has a life of its own.

It may be needed and wanted to move
our humanity forward by
entertaining us and bring us joy,
or by profoundly inspiring us
to effect change on the planet.

Whatever the dream,
it IS the reflection
of your heart's desires.

So Dream.

Dream upon a Star.

And wait.

Wait because you know,
somewhere deep within,
that it will come true.

Villa & Jardins Ephrussi de Rothchild
St. Jean-Cap-Ferrat, France

Sunken Garden, Butchart Gardens
Brentwood Bay, British Columbia, Canada

Wishing you
a bright
and
sunny day.

May cheer
and
pleasure be
yours.

Blessings dear ones.

Dream infinitely grand.

The power of
your thoughts
can produce a world
you wish for
in those dreams.

Then wait.

Watch.

Do you see
where it has become
your reality?

San Francisco Bay
Oakland Hills, California

Blessings dear ones.

When is enough, simply that, "enough"?

When is enough money, enough?

When is enough power, enough?

When is enough happiness, enough?

When is enough recognition, enough?

When is enough . . . , enough?

When the *whole* within us is filled with
our knowing of ourselves
as extraordinary beings,
precious and uniquely worthy,
all else will require very little
to be sufficient,
plenty,
and as much as necessary
to render it Enough.

Blessings on your fully filled life,
dear ones.

Crystal clear is the heart

that expresses authentic truth.

Sunken Garden, Butchart Gardens
Brentwood Bay, British Columbia, Canada

The Blossoming of *Anew.*

The birds are singing.

Their melody welcoming
the freshness in the air.

The days have grown longer.

The flurry of movement
can be sensed on the streets.

It's coming.

It's almost upon us.

It's doors are slowly opening
in our direction.

The new day, the new season,
the new life which arises
with the splendor of

Spring.

The golden rays of this morning's

Welcome.

The opening for a new adventure

Awaits.

Arise to this day,
uninterrupted by yesterday
nor
focusing upon tomorrow.

Give allowance
for a mystical moment
to unveil itSelf for

You.

Valle dei Templi
Agrigento AG, Italy

Blessings upon the miraculous,
dear ones.

Abundance arises from
giving of yourself
to another.

When you set out
to have others win,
genuinely focused
on the rise of
another's greatness,
the cycle of giving
finds itself at your door

Naturally.

Our Global Family
is in the
palm of our hands.

We have been entrusted with all of it,
to hold and handle it with care
for the generations coming
after our own.

For those we will never meet,
never know.

Those beings are counting on us
as we did on our ancestors to
tenderly move,
thoughtfully behave,
and courageously act.

WE

ARE

ONE.

Eze, Côte d'Azur, France

What does the quiet of mind, stillness of spirit, calming heart produce?

An empty space to create anything.

Riomaggiore, Cinque Terre, Italy

There is a space
—a moment—
between a particular impact
and our response,
and it's called
Choice.

We have the remarkable power,
inherent within us,
to consciously choose
our response to a situation
rather than act from auto pilot.

From this space, freedom is possible,
new results are possible,
life is possible.

Blessings to you dear ones.

The beauty and gift of our life
is that we have another day.

Always new,
always waiting freshly for our embrace
without the burden of yesterday
or worry of tomorrow.

Today,
this day,
is yours and yours alone
to create newly
from new thoughts,
arising from a new state of being.

What will you create, newly, today?

Blessings upon your freshly embraced day,
dear ones.

Tempio di Segesta
Calatafimi-Segesta, Sicily

About the

Author

Banafsheh Akhlaghi is a pioneering civil and human rights attorney, educator and social entrepreneur. She has learned through her work how decisions we make globally affect us locally and has always worked to transform lives at all levels.

She immigrated to the United States from her native Iran with her parents at the age of five. As a child, she sat at her father's side as he recited poems of Hafez and other great poets, experiencing the magic and passion of the words and sharing. Like her fellow countrymen, she too learned to engage the world on all levels through the living language of the poets. This perspective has influenced every aspect of her life, inspiring her to grab hold of every opportunity, reach for every dream and push for justice and peace every day.

She started her career as a professor of Constitutional Law at the John F. Kennedy University College of Law. Banafsheh has worked as a consultant with the United Nations Development Fund for Women (UNIFEM) and was the director of the West Region for Amnesty International.

She has won several awards for her work, including the Fred Korematsu Civil Rights Award. Banafsheh was named one of the "Top 100 Leading Lawyers in California" and "Top 100 Most Influential Lawyers in California" by the Daily Journal.

She was also nominated for the Robert F. Kennedy Human Rights Award in 2008 and received a Certificate of Special Congressional Recognition from the U.S. House of Representatives that same year. She has spoken at conferences and events around the world, met with world leaders, thinkers, artists and activists, and has dedicated her life to the realization of peace in her lifetime.

Banafsheh received her B.A. from the University of San Francisco, with attendance at Cambridge University, and her J.D. from Tulane University.

Resources

During my travels I found myself wanting to memorialize particular moments, feelings or moods as I felt myself drawn to a message from mother earth or a memory gone-by.

Sometimes, the prose is inspired by the photos, while at other times the prose inspires the photos. There is a dance of sorts between the two. I hope you enjoy these captured moments and allow them to transport you to another time and place, while remaining grounded in the here and now.

I am not a professional photographer. I only used the pure and natural light of the moment and the object of the image before me. Each photo in this book was captured on my handheld phone.

Blessings to you dear ones.

All photographs were produced and are owned by the author.

The *Beautiful Reminders* journey continues with book two expected to release by the end of 2015.

Check back regularly to find additional offerings.

Visit us at www.BeautifulReminders.com.

Beautiful Reminders Book 2

will be available in
2015

Made in the USA
Lexington, KY
11 April 2015